How Can I Help?

Friends Helping Friend

HELPING A FRIEND WITH A DRUG PROBLEM

Precious McKenzie

ROSEN
PUBLISHING

New York

Published in 2017 by The Rosen Publishing Group, Inc.
29 East 21st Street, New York, NY 10010

Library of Congress Cataloging-in-Publication Data

Names: McKenzie, Precious, 1975– author.
Title: Helping a friend with a drug problem / Precious McKenzie.
Description: New York : Rosen Publishing, 2017. | Series: How can i help?: Friends helping friends | Includes bibliographical references and index.
Identifiers: LCCN 2016018356| ISBN 9781499464467 (library bound) | ISBN 9781499464443 (pbk.) | ISBN 9781499464450 (6-pack)
Subjects: LCSH: Drug abuse—Juvenile literature. | Drug addiction—Juvenile literature.
Classification: LCC HV5809.5 .M35 2017 | DDC 362.29/18—dc23

LC record available at https://lccn.loc.gov/2016018356

Manufactured in the United States of America

CONTENTS

INTRODUCTION

It's the weekend—time to forget about school, have fun, and unwind. Your friend invites you to a house party. When you get there, you immediately begin having fun, talking, and enjoying the music. But then you realize some of the people are smoking pot. They offer some to you and your friend. You refuse, but your friend says yes, and smokes some. Your friend's behavior soon changes. It's not long before all you want to do is get your friend out of there as quickly as possible.

In 2014, almost 20 percent of teens had smoked marijuana at some point during their high school years. In 2012, 40 percent of twelfth graders reported using at least one type of drug. Yet, drug use among teens is actually on the decline, compared to twenty years ago. Specifically, high school students have decreased their alcohol consumption. According to the 2015 Monitoring the Future Study, a reported 58 percent of twelfth graders have used alcohol whereas 34 percent have smoked marijuana. But that study found that marijuana use remained steady in the high school population.

Although the reported drug use numbers are going down, teens are still highly susceptible to abusing extremely dangerous drugs. In fact, if a person tried drugs as a teen, then that person is more likely to become a drug user as an adult.

Unlike the scenario above, drug use isn't just happening at parties. Drugs are circulating at school and in neighborhoods—and at alarming rates. For example, a Huffington Post article reports almost 60 percent of high school students see their high schools as "drug infested," and almost

This assortment of controlled substances shows many of the forms of drugs and ways to consume them.

17 percent of those surveyed reported using drugs during the day. According to a 2012 study by the National Center on Addiction and Substance Abuse at Columbia University, 44 percent of students know someone who sells drugs. Most of those respondents said marijuana is the most commonly sold drug at school (91 percent), followed by prescription drugs (24 percent), cocaine (9 percent), and ecstasy (7 percent).

More likely than not, in your teen years, someone will offer you or your friends drugs. If you have a friend who does develop a drug problem, there are steps you can take to recognize it. There are ways to address the situation, and teams of professionals who are ready to assist.

CHAPTER ONE

WHAT DOES ADDICTION LOOK LIKE?

Teens often experiment with tobacco, alcohol, marijuana, and other drugs. If they try it once and never do it again, that's not addiction.

Any recreational use of drugs—even experimentation—can be deadly. But even if the experiments don't result in death, a person who experiments with drugs often goes on to become a casual user, and possibly even an addict. If a friend becomes a user, it's good to know what to do and when to step in and ask for help. So it's important to know the differences between casual use, addiction, and dependency.

DEFINING ADDICTION

Casual drug use is when people use drugs for nonmedical, or recreational, reasons. But they do not use it to excess, and they can control their urges for the drug. Recreational use that falls out of bounds of a legal drug's purpose is considered misuse, and is therefore referred to as substance abuse. Any use of an illegal drug is also considered substance abuse.

Addiction is another form of recreational use, but with none of the self-control of the casual substance abuser. While casual users feel that they are in control, it cannot be stressed enough that the casual user typically slips unintentionally into addiction. Similarly, dependence is when a user's neurological function cannot be normal without the substance. The distinction is between self-control (present in casual use and possibly present in dependency) and no control (the cornerstone of addiction and may be present in dependency).

The intense craving one gets from being away from drugs is the cornerstone of addiction. This makes it hard to focus on anything else.

Drug addiction is serious, so much so that it is considered a disease. Specifically, addiction is a disease of obsession. People with an addiction feel like they cannot live without the drug, and this may be true in the presence of withdrawal. This sense of desperation leads to some very negative behavioral changes.

In addiction, physical dependence usually happens in tandem with psychological addiction. Physical dependence is when the body reacts badly to not having the drug, whether the body consumes too little of it, or none. In the human brain, neurotransmitters send messages via chemicals that travel across synapses from one cell to another. When a person takes drugs, the chemicals in the drugs interact with the brain's neurotransmitters to alter the way a person feels, moves, sees, and hears. The measurement of tolerance helps to define the extent of physical dependence and refers to the levels of the drug that the body requires in order to feel its effect. A person's body will develop tolerance to a drug over time so that more of the drug is needed to get high or relieve pain. This causes a strengthening of the body's dependence on the drug because a high tolerance means a longer-lasting disturbance of neurological processes that only the drug can even out.

Psychological addiction happens when the chemicals in drugs alter a person's mental state such that the user prioritizes getting high over all else. Once the high from a drug is over, the user wants the drug so he can get back to that high. Naturally, this desire manifests itself in the user acting toward acquiring that drug, or money to buy it. An especially desperate user will act without regard for consequences in the pursuit of getting high, and possibly without attempting to hide that he is pursuing drugs.

When the body doesn't consume enough of the drug, physical and psychological withdrawal occurs. Withdrawal can be mild to severe, and varies based on the level of dependency on the drug. Part of withdrawal is that the addict's brain is readapting to the changing chemicals in the brain. Sometimes a person will develop shaking, depression, anxiety, racing heartbeat, excessive sweating, nausea, diarrhea, and headaches, among other symptoms. More serious withdrawal symptoms include seizures, hallucinations, heart attacks, and strokes.

SPOTTING SIGNS OF ADDICTION

It can be hard to spot substance abuse and addiction. Some high-functioning drug addicts manage to hide their substance abuse and its signs, leaving little for people in their lives to recognize. However, it is often the case that substance abuse and drug addiction causes changes in a person's behavior, so if your friend begins to act differently, that is a sign. A change in behavior in just one day could be caused by a variety of issues. But if your friend was normally social, had good grades, and was involved with hobbies or activities but isn't interested in those things anymore, that might signal a drug problem. Does she seem depressed? Is she skipping school? Is she hanging out with a new crowd? Many drastic changes like this are clear signs of trouble.

Teens who are there for each other are more likely to recognize signs that something is wrong.

ALCOHOL

Alcohol abuse is one of the most common problems among teens. It is often one of the most deadly. Alcohol affects a person's coordination and memory. Drinkers report feeling relaxed or even sleepy. Alcohol slows down a person's reflexes and functioning and impairs judgment and coordination. Thousands of teens each year get hurt or killed in accidents related to alcohol use.

Alcohol content varies from drink to drink. A beer might be made up of from as low as 3 to as high as 10 percent alcohol and whiskey might be made up of 40 to 50 percent alcohol. Therefore, it would take less whiskey to make a person feel drunk. But, beer and wine are not "safer" to drink than whiskey and other types of liquor.

There's a difference between social drinking and addiction. A person addicted to or dependent on alcohol drinks large quantities frequently. He or she might not be able to cut down on drinking or give it up. Or he or she might participate in risky behaviors such as having unprotected sex with multiple partners. An alcohol-dependent person might drink and drive, endangering herself and others. But these are risks that come with many types of drug abuse and addiction.

MARIJUANA

After alcohol, marijuana is the most commonly used drug by teens. The Washington State Healthy Youth Study of 2012 reported that 19 percent of tenth graders and 27 percent of

Spice, or synthetic marijuana, looks like this before being ground up for sale and use. Like marijuana, it is usually smoked.

twelfth graders used marijuana. Across the United States, 45 percent of teens reported using marijuana at least once, according to the 2012 Monitoring the Future (MTF) Study.

Researchers have found that marijuana causes memory and cognitive problems and balance and coordination problems. It also has been linked to increased absences from school and poorer academic performance.

If you have a friend who uses marijuana frequently, he or she might have slow reaction time, appear spaced out, or act paranoid. Your friend may be forgetful and have memory problems. There are other signs to look out for, such as red eyes, goofy behavior, uncontrollable giggling, sleepiness, and lots of snacking. Marijuana also has a distinct smell. Law enforcement officers describe the smell as sweeter than tobacco or skunky. If you smell a strange odor like that on your friend, it could be marijuana.

Another drug often associated with marijuana is Spice. Spice is a blend of shredded plant material and chemicals. Spice also goes by the names K2, Bliss, Yucatan Fire, Genie, Bombay Blue, or Skunk. Drug sellers label Spice as synthetic marijuana since Spice doesn't contain marijuana. In fact, Spice is much stronger than marijuana. Drug sellers also claim that Spice is all natural, but it is not. It is filled with man-made chemicals. These blends cause unpredictable and extremely dangerous highs.

Along with the relaxed feeling of a typical marijuana high, a Spice high can also be accompanied by some severe and very visible symptoms: vomiting, hallucinations, blurred vision, seizures, and even cardiac arrest. To recognize if a friend is high on Spice, look for red eyes, paranoia, panic attacks, talk of numbness and tingling, aggression, inability to speak, unconsciousness, or complaints of a very high heart rate. Another way to recognize Spice use is by witnessing withdrawal symptoms. Those that a friend can see include extreme sweating, psychotic episodes, indifference toward consequences, loss of appetite, and loss of motivation. A teen who is withdrawing may express suicidal thoughts or indicate that he is depressed.

Another drug that is associated with marijuana is butane hash oil (BHO). Unlike synthetic marijuana, BHO is a derivative of marijuana. Users place part of BHO on a hot metal surface and inhale the fumes. BHO is much stronger than marijuana and usually knocks users unconscious.

Symptoms of BHO use involve slowing down. A BHO user has trouble concentrating, impaired coordination and judgment, slowed speech, and a lowered ability to communicate or think clearly. BHO users also suffer drowsiness, poor short-term memory, and lowered inhibitions. Physical signs include snacking, red eyes, and dry mouth.

INHALANTS

Anyone can buy inhalants—just walk into a grocery store. Inhalants are chemicals that are intentionally breathed or snorted in with the intent to get high. There are more than one thousand products that can, when used improperly, be considered inhalants. Glue, felt-tip markers, spray paint, nail polish, and hair spray are a few that can cause long-term brain and nerve damage, coughing, difficulty breathing, and a bluish color on the user's arms and legs.

Like marijuana, inhalants cause sleepiness and slow reflexes. Inhalants also cause dizziness, muscle weakness, seizures, and unconsciousness. Inhalant abuse and its signs can be harder to spot on a friend. People tend to huff the chemicals alone and never tell anyone that they are abusing inhalants.

The signs of inhalant abuse are easy to recognize, even if you are unsure if your friend is addicted. If your friend complains of bad headaches, has shaky hands, coughs often, is nauseous, or acts anxious or excited, he or she may be using inhalants to get high. Users also have sores around the mouth, along with red or runny eyes from inhaling the poisonous fumes.

COCAINE AND CRACK

Cocaine comes from the leaves of the coca plant, and it is grown in South America. In its pure form, cocaine is a white powder. Users sniff, or snort, cocaine to get high. Crack cocaine, on the other hand, is shaped like large crystals, and is usually white or pinkish yellow in color.

Cocaine and crack are extremely addictive. Regardless of its form, cocaine is a stimulant that causes the brain to be flooded with dopamine. When people use these drugs, they feel extremely energetic and euphoric. These drugs speed up a person's entire system, including blood pressure and heart rate. People who use crack and cocaine often develop a tolerance, causing them to desire more of the drug than when they initially started.

People who use cocaine seem hyperactive and talkative. But they also have tremors, numbness, anxiety, and paranoia. Cocaine use leads to increased chances of stroke, heart attack, hallucinations, convulsions, heart failure, and respiratory arrest, resulting in death.

HEROIN AND OPIOIDS

Opioids and heroin come from the opium poppy plant. Opioids are strong pain-killing drugs. Someone dependent on them must have the drug every eight to twelve hours in order to avoid severe withdrawal. Opioid and heroin use can cost users over $200 a day.

According to a 2013 article in *Teen Vogue*, "How Heroin Is Invading America's Schools," heroin, once the injectable drug of choice in poor urban areas, has now become available in pill form and has spread to the suburbs. Users open the pill and snort it. Most people who get hooked on heroin were first hooked on prescription pain pills, opioids such as OxyContin, Vicodin, Percocet, or Fentanyl. With the rising cost of these pills, users turn to less expensive heroin pills to get the same kind of high.

Around 2002, a new drug popped up in Russia. Krokodil, or desomorphine, is a deadly blend of codeine, paint thinner, gasoline, and hydrochloric acid, among other ingredients. Krokodil is injected into a vein, like heroin.

Prescription drugs are becoming the most abused drugs in the United States. They often serve as a gateway drug to heroin.

It gets its name from the scaly, green effect it leaves on the user's skin. The person's skin begins to look like the skin of a crocodile. Using Krokodil leads to skin abscesses, gangrene, and amputations. Users' skin rots off and leaves bare bone. Krokodil is highly habit forming, to the point where users aspire to inject themselves with the drug every ninety minutes. Doctors report that getting off of Krokodil is extremely painful and probably the most difficult recovery they've ever seen.

Law enforcement has seen the spread of Krokodil to the United States. In 2011, police and law enforcement confiscated sixty-five million doses of Krokodil in the first three months of the year.

Heroin and opioid abuse leave telltale signs for family and friends of users. The most common side effects are itchy skin, nausea, flushed skin, and throwing up. Users skip school, constantly need money, and they stop taking care of personal hygiene.

AMPHETAMINES AND METHAMPHETAMINES

Once used only for medical purposes, today teens and young adults use amphetamines and methamphetamines recreationally and for performance enhancement.

Amphetamines are drugs that help people stay awake and alert. Doctors prescribe amphetamines to narcoleptics. In the past, the military had fighter pilots take amphetamines in order to help them stay alert. But now, they are used in ADHD prescription medications such as Adderall. In addition to that usage, athletes and students illegally obtain and use amphetamines and quickly become addicted to the

UNINTENDED CONSEQUENCES

Opioid addiction is becoming more and more common in the United States. According to *Rolling Stone* magazine, since 2000, deaths from opioids have tripled. OxyContin, Vicodin, Percocet, and Fentanyl, in particular, are often prescribed by doctors after a surgery or injury has occurred because they help ease the pain. However, they can quickly and easily lead to dependence and addiction.

Musician Macklemore has been open about his past addiction to opioids. He was fortunate enough to get treatment, but he lost a good friend to an opioid overdose. Macklemore is working with President Obama to ask Congress to increase regulations on opioid prescriptions and also increase funding for substance abuse treatment centers so more people can get the treatment that they need.

alertness they feel while taking the drug. Since Adderall suppresses the appetite, another reason for amphetamine use is that the user wants to lose weight.

There are some typical signs that can give away if someone is abusing amphetamines. Someone who appears to be hostile or paranoid, in addition to having little or no appetite, may be high on amphetamines. Other highly noticeable signs include dilated pupils, euphoria, faster, shallow breathing, nausea, hallucinations, and convulsions.

Meth has spread rapidly across the United States, even reaching into small, rural communities. Meth is an addictive stimulant made from deadly ingredients like antifreeze and battery acid. Meth comes in different forms, usually powder or chunks, but sometimes pills. It is usually white or yellow, but it can be green or brown.

People take methamphetamines because they want the rush and the high that is unique to meth. Unlike amphetamines, and in spite of their similar impact and composition, meth is thought of as a strictly recreational drug.

Look for these signs to help determine if a friend is using meth: extreme alertness, increased confidence, intense sexual desire, thoughts of indestructibleness, euphoria, extreme energy. The friend's high might last from eight to fifteen hours. A meth user craves more of the drug. A user will binge on meth and stay awake for days at a time getting high. Then the user crashes. The user becomes exhausted, irritable, anxious, depressed, even violent or paranoid. The user might hallucinate or hear voices. Or the user might scratch himself because his skin feels itchy. Meth causes memory loss, kidney damage, brain damage, insomnia, lung damage, and convulsions. Meth users quickly become fixated on the drug and ignore the rest of the world, including their friends, families, school, and hobbies. All they want to do is use meth again and again. If your friend exhibits any of these symptoms, don't wait—you must seek help before meth kills your friend.

HALLUCINOGENS

A class of illicit drugs, hallucinogens contain psychoactive chemicals that cause strange sensations, hallucinations, and bizarre dreams. Users of hallucinogens see colors vividly or hear and taste things stronger than they ever have before.

Some hallucinogens come from plants, such as mescaline and psilocybin. Others are made in labs or in a drug dealer's home or garage. LSD, ketamine, and ecstasy are all man-made substances. All of them are dangerous because of the intense trips they cause. Taken in high enough quantities, hallucinogens can cause respiratory problems and possibly death.

How can you tell if a friend has used a hallucinogen? His eyes may be dilated. He might sweat profusely, have a fast heartbeat, and have goosebumps. The most obvious sign is if he suffers hallucinations.

IT CAN HAPPEN TO ANYONE

In spite of laws and common protective practices, drugs and addiction are such multifaceted problems that even infants are able to become victims. If a mother-to-be is addicted to a drug, her baby is likely to develop dependence on that drug. A baby in such circumstances is at the mercy of his or her support system to recognize the potential for a damaging, or even fatal, withdrawal experience. Or in many cases, children who find themselves in unhealthy environments may experiment with drugs voluntarily or unknowingly, causing themselves to face the same threat of the vulnerable infant.

Adults are likely to be exposed to drugs in similar contexts as teens: from friends, in casual settings like parties and concerts, and through their own efforts to seek the drug of choice. But once an addiction begins, it manifests itself differently for these two age groups. For instance, an adult with a drug problem has different forms of pressure and different stakes. An adult's drug addiction encompasses a struggle with financial problems, possibly resulting in losing a job and even becoming homeless. Failing a drug test can have serious consequences, like termination of employment. A teen, on the other hand, may lose her grip on her social environment. Worse yet, teens and younger children are most at risk for addiction because their brains are still developing, and are thus fairly malleable.

MYTHS AND FACTS

MYTH: Only illegal drugs, such as cocaine and meth, are addictive.

FACT: Drugs don't have to be illegal to be addictive. Alcohol, tobacco, and prescription drugs can be just as addictive as illicit drugs. And just as deadly, too.

MYTH: Only bored or depressed people try drugs.

FACT: A person doesn't have to be depressed or bored to try drugs. People experiment with drugs for a wide variety of reasons. Sometimes, doing drugs is a choice someone makes. Other times, someone makes that choice for someone else.

MYTH: After a person has completed treatment, a drug problem will never return.

FACT: After treatment, some people remain sober for the rest of their lives. Other people return to using drugs and will need additional rehabilitation.

CHAPTER TWO

WHY DO FRIENDS TURN TO DRUGS?

People turn to drugs for a variety of reasons. Some of these reasons have to do with one's environment, and others have to do with internal forces. Being aware of the circumstances of a friend's life can help you to understand that addiction doesn't just happen—it's a sequence of events that should, once recognized, be steered in a healthy direction.

SOCIAL REASONS

As a teenager gets to know herself, she will have to face social situations that she isn't necessarily prepared for. High school, and even middle school are places where people learn to interact with each other, in addition to the academic lessons they learn from teachers. Unfortunately, these are also the places where teens are first exposed to drugs. Here are some reasons that teens typically don't say no to drugs.

EXPERIMENTATION

Some of your friends may want to try something different, so they turn to drugs to see what will happen. A friend might

Teens at a music festival often encounter situations in which they are offered drugs. At an outdoor venue like this, there might be people selling their supply.

watch a group of people get high at a party and decide it looks like fun. That person may join the activity to try the drug for the first time. It can quickly become a tragic medical emergency or a full-blown addiction.

Or a drug dealer may offer a sample of a drug, perhaps a joint of marijuana. Giving potential customers a sample of a drug is an easy and effective way to get someone hooked on that drug drug later on—this is a phenomenon called grooming with gateway drugs. After the first taste of the drug, a person who wants more starts to buy the drug regularly from the drug dealer. The spiral of addiction works such that someone who thinks of herself as a casual user starts to look for new or more intense highs. She becomes more willing

HOW TO PROTECT YOURSELF AND YOUR FRIENDS

Illicit drugs might be odorless and tasteless. A friend wouldn't know just from looking at her drink that someone spiked it with ecstasy. Your friend might not have intended ever to do ecstasy but, because of this, she has just ingested an illicit substance. When a friend's drink has been spiked, your friend becomes an easy target for crime. She might get raped, assaulted, or robbed because she has lost all of her senses. A recent survey of 150,000 college students across twenty-seven universities provided data on the relationship between drug and alcohol use and sexual assault and rape. Among female students, 23 percent reported that they experienced unwanted sexual contact after they had used alcohol or drugs. Many of these women knew the person who attacked them. Other nationwide surveys cite that one out of five women will have to deal with sexual assault or rape after using drugs. Drugs impair a person's level of awareness, and this can put a person in extreme danger.

But there are ways to protect yourself and your friends before it comes to that.

Tips:
- Limit or do not drink alcohol.
- Do not accept drinks from strangers.
- Do not set your drink down or leave it unattended.
- Avoid drinks served in communal bowls or containers.
- If your drink tastes salty, bitter, or strange, stop drinking it.

to graduate to harder, more expensive, and more addictive drugs like crystal meth.

PEER PRESSURE

Teens spend a lot of time with friends. In fact, a teen's friends are the single most important social group in high school, more than family. Teens will usually try just about anything to fit in or act cool or be part of the in-crowd.

If your friend wants to fit in or look cool, then he might be easily pressured into trying drugs. A friend with low self-confidence or low self-esteem will take drugs if the dominant, popular crowd pressures him into it. Likewise, drug dealers prey on kids with low self-confidence because they are easy targets.

PSYCHOLOGICAL REASONS

Often linked with social influences, internal forces in teen's lives often cause them to seek relief. The following are some situations that might lead teens to finding a desire for, or a solution in, drugs.

DEPRESSION, LONELINESS, BOREDOM

Although there are other psychological disorders that can lead to drug abuse, the most common one is depression. People who are depressed look for ways to feel better. They may turn to uppers or speed to make them feel a euphoric high, even if it is only for a short time. Or they may turn to illegally acquired prescription painkillers like opioids to mask the pain they are feeling inside.

Loneliness and boredom are especially hard for teens to deal with. Teens like to socialize, make friends, and feel like they belong. If one of your friends feels left out of your group or frequently feels bored, she might turn to drugs to ease the pain of being alone or to pass the time.

PEAK PERFORMANCE

High-achieving students can be just as easily tempted to become drug abusers as well. This temptation stems from questioning whether or not an athlete or student is able to improve his or her performance any further through natural means, or believing that other athletes have an advantage that a potential drug abuser must overcome. Amphetamines, steroids, and performance enhancers all amp up a person's bodily functions. These drugs can make people feel more powerful and motivated.

Similarly, illegally acquiring and using prescription ADD medication among college students has been on the rise in the United States since 2006. The reason is that high-achieving college students feel intense pressure to get high grades and meet tight deadlines for projects. This medication makes them feel energized and motivated.

Athletes and dancers also turn to amphetamines and other performance enhancers in order to stay at the top of their game. Ballet dancers, who are praised for being lithe and thin, have been known to take diet pills, speed, and amphetamines to help them lose weight and remain thin.

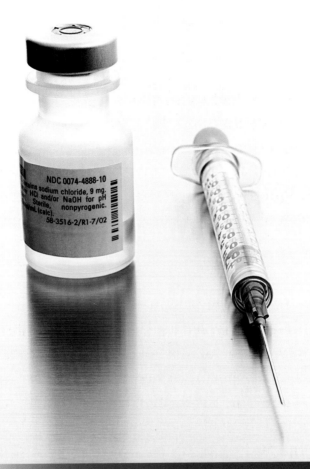

Performance-enhancing drugs, like steroids, are banned from many competitive sporting events. If a professional athlete is caught, she could be banned from the sport.

Wrestlers, too, have used amphetamines to help them stay in a particular weight range for competition. School administrators know the temptation of performance-enhancing drugs and often utilize drug screening in highly competitive athletic leagues to deter substance abuse.

10 GREAT QUESTIONS TO ASK A GUIDANCE COUNSELOR

1 WHAT IS THE DIFFERENCE BETWEEN CASUAL DRUG USE AND ADDICTION?

2 HOW CAN I TELL IF A FRIEND HAS A DRUG PROBLEM?

3 SHOULD I TALK TO MY FRIEND'S PARENTS?

4 SHOULD I TALK TO LAW ENFORCEMENT ABOUT THE DRUG PROBLEM?

5 WHAT CAN I DO TO HELP MY FRIEND STOP USING DRUGS?

6 WHAT CAN THE SCHOOL DO TO HELP FIGHT ILLICIT DRUGS?

7 WHAT COMMUNITY RESOURCES ARE AVAILABLE TO HELP MY FRIEND?

8 WHAT TYPES OF THERAPY OR COUNSELING ARE AVAILABLE NEARBY?

9 HOW CAN I HELP MY FRIEND AVOID DRUGS?

10 WHERE CAN I GO TO GET HELP FOR MYSELF AS MY FRIEND DEALS WITH HIS DRUG PROBLEM?

CHAPTER THREE

HOW CAN YOU FIGHT A DRUG PROBLEM?

Once you discover a friend has a drug problem, you'll probably want to help end it. But before you can do that, your friend has to recognize that there is a problem. When everybody's on the same page, it will be easier to decide on an action plan that will end the addiction.

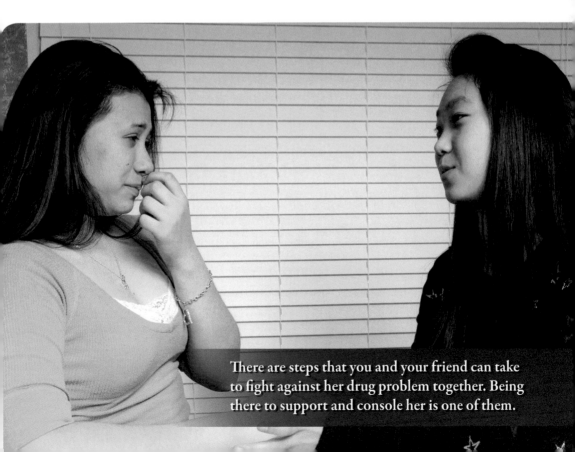

There are steps that you and your friend can take to fight against her drug problem together. Being there to support and console her is one of them.

HELP RECOGNIZE THE PROBLEM

Bringing attention to a drug problem can happen in a few ways. As the person who recognizes the problem, you may feel compelled to talk about it with your friend. Similarly, your friend's parents or other friends may recognize what is wrong, and they may also confront the friend. Another way that a drug problem gains recognition is through honest self-reflection.

TALK ABOUT CHANGE BUT DON'T PREACH

The Hazelden Betty Ford Foundation gives advice on how to talk to someone who is using drugs. These means of confronting the drug abuser are the same for friends and concerned parents or other authority figures, but the conversation may change based on the relationship dynamic of those involved.

First and foremost: it is important that you initiate a talk about your friend's drug use when your friend is sober. It may be difficult to coordinate a chat at a time when you know your friend isn't high. And your friend may not always exhibit recognizable signs when high. But if you have noticed a pattern of abuse, you may be able to take advantage of your knowledge to figure out when would be best to talk.

Choose a convenient time and a quiet place that will give you both the type of space you need to focus. Don't talk about it in public, as that may cause embarrassment or allow distractions to end the conversation. And make sure that you both have a good amount of time for the discussion, so that you can face each other in a way that will allow you to express all of your concerns.

When you do meet, be careful not to criticize. Discuss drug addiction like the disease it is, not some shortcoming that you should hang over the head of your friend. Don't blame. Don't preach. One of the best ways to have this conversation is to be specific. Use "I" phrases to describe your feelings. Say things like, "I'm concerned about" or "I'm worried about." A good friend will not be able to argue with your feelings, especially if you sound caring and concerned. Also, point out how the drug use affects what your friend cares most about—family, school, sports, or whatever that something is in your friend's life.

TRACK DRUG USE

People who use drugs usually don't think they have a problem. When confronted about drug use, they will lie or deny how often they use drugs. They might be scared or ashamed of their use. Or they may not realize how the drug is taking over their lives. Regardless of if your friend recognizes the drug problem, ask your friend to track his drug use. Let him know that you don't need to see that record because it's only for him. As he keeps a log of the days and times he uses drugs over the course of a month, he can see for himself how often he turns to drugs.

The reason he should track his drug use even if he does recognize the problem is that a record will help determine if there is a pattern to his drug use. How often does he get high, and how long does each high last? How much does

Drug abuse has a particularly bad impact on relationships. Speaking to a drug addict about her problem doesn't always end with the most favorable result.

he use? Does he use drugs when he's stressed out or bored? Does he use drugs just at parties? Or only with certain friends? There could also be trigger situations that spark a friend's drug use that tracking will allow your friend to see more clearly. When your friend identifies the patterns, it is often easier to change them or prepare for or avoid trigger situations.

Tracking drug use requires that your friend be honest with himself. He must faithfully record each time he takes a drug. Otherwise, tracking is a means of denial. More importantly, your friend will never receive effective help until he admits his problem to himself.

SPOTTING ADDICTION

According to Project Know, these questions will help you determine if your friend has a drug problem. If your friend answers yes to these questions, that's a good indication that a drug problem exists.

Have you ever been in a car with someone who was drunk or high? Have you ever driven a car while you were drunk or high?

Do you use drugs to relax or hang out and fit in with your friends?

Do you use drugs when you are alone?

Do you black out after drinking or using drugs?

Have your family and friends ever told you that they think you have a problem?

Have you ever gotten into trouble because of drugs or alcohol?

FORMING AN ACTION PLAN

Once your friend is ready to receive help, creating an action plan will put him on the path to recovery. You'll want to decide on some clear, actionable goals. While working on these goals, if you listen to your friend when he wants to talk, you'll offer much-needed emotional support because your friend won't have to fight his drug problem alone.

MAKE GOALS

Medical experts agree that goal setting can be the key to kicking a drug habit. Quitting all at once, or "going cold turkey," is a tough goal and can even be unadvisable for certain classes of drugs, like opioids. Goals don't have to be large or hard to reach at first. Help your friend decide on an achievable goal. A good first step would be setting a goal like "I won't smoke weed today." Take note as your friend gradually increases the time between taking the drug, going from one day to two and then to three.

If a person has a drug problem, it is hard to resist the temptation of drugs. It is often the case that a person's drug problem is multifaceted—in other words, involving multiple drugs. People with drug problems remember and crave the high feeling they got from using drugs, so there are many situations that may be dangerous to the recovery process. You can offer support by making a sobriety pledge. Be sober together in every possible way. Don't take your friend to parties, concerts, or other places where drug use happens and encourage your friend to find hobbies or activities to do together that don't involve drugs.

Goals don't have to be only about drugs. It could be good for your friend to work toward repairing whatever damage his drug habit has caused to his social life. This may include committing to repairing old friendships or getting back into old hobbies. Having a friend to help with this process can make it easier.

PHYSIOLOGICAL AND SOCIAL CONSEQUENCES

Drug use can have lasting effects on a person's brain and body. Brain functioning can be impaired or destroyed by drug abuse. Users of LSD and other hallucinogens can have flashbacks years after using the drug. Researchers are also beginning to study drug abuse in conjunction with mental illness. They are trying to determine if hallucinogens might be linked to schizophrenia. But they are sure that some drugs cause various forms of permanent brain damage, such as difficulty processing information, short-term and long-term memory loss, and spatial disorientation.

In addition to wreaking havoc on the brain and central nervous system, drug use impairs lung, kidney, and liver functioning. Marijuana has been found to increase the odds of sterility or infertility. Meth use causes skin sores and loss of hair and teeth. Teens who use drugs are at an increased risk for suicide, homicide, and accidental death.

Drug use destroys social networks and social lives, too. Drug users stop finding pleasure in their once-favorite pastimes. They stop hanging around with their non–drug using friends. Very often, they start to hang around with other users or dealers as they seek

(continued on the next page)

(continued from the previous page)

out their next high. Drug users withdraw from their families, most of the time to hide the underlying problem of drug addiction. Worse yet, drug users may turn to crime in order to pay for their habits. Studies have found that teens who use drugs are more likely to commit crimes or acts of violence than teens who do not use drugs.

Because a teen who is high is more likely to engage in unprotected sex, teens who use drugs also report higher levels of STDs and HIV.

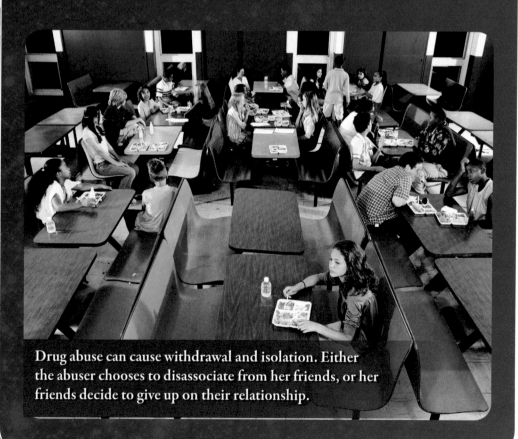

Drug abuse can cause withdrawal and isolation. Either the abuser chooses to disassociate from her friends, or her friends decide to give up on their relationship.

BE THERE TO LISTEN

Things will begin to change in your friend's life when she and those around her begin to acknowledge that she has a problem. Each person in her family will interact in new ways with her or on her behalf when faced with substance abuse. Parents often deny that their child has a problem and try to protect the child from the consequences of the child's actions. Parents sometimes try to solve the situation by loosening the reins on their child. When they do this, they hope the child interprets their actions as meaning that they are more loving or accepting of the person. Or parents might become extra strict and set harsher rules and punishments as a way to control and buckle down on their teen. Instead of enabling or punishing, parents need to set boundaries and teach the teen to take personal responsibility to overcome the drug problem. Regardless of how it goes, the beginning of acknowledging the problem is an extremely emotional and tense situation that tests family relationships.

But, according to the Hazelden Betty Ford Foundation, families of drug users are often not the ones most able to intervene. Friends are the ones who can make the most impact in helping a buddy get off drugs. A friend will need you the most through the whole process, from bringing up the subject of drug abuse to being available during the recovery. Your friend will need to vent, complain, maybe even scream, shout, or cry. Your friend will need a nonjudgmental listener to help talk out her frustration. Your friend will appreciate

A supportive group of friends is a great alternative to giving in to the temptation of drugs. Helping your friend to move in a positive direction will make a big difference.

if you call every once in a while to check in on her, and she will be happy to know that you're available if she needs you.

But know your limits. Moral support can be taxing, and you may also realize that you're not sure about the appropriate response to your own or your friend's feelings or actions. And, you may not want to always be on-call when your friend needs help with a problem. Seeking help, or suggesting that your friend find someone who is more available at a particular time when a situation arises with which your friend needs help can lead to better outcomes. And, it's good to know that there are other people you can rely on when there's a lot of pressure in a situation.

CHAPTER FOUR

TURNING TO THE PROFESSIONALS

Professional teams of doctors, therapists, and social workers have experience treating people with drug problems. They make a big difference in the recovery process. Unfortunately, you can't make your friend get help from professionals. He has to decide to do this on his own, unless a parent decides that your friend should start treatment. But you can encourage your friend to contact professionals, and you can make your friend's problem known to your friend's parents. While it may not be safe for you to keep your friend's secret, your friend can take comfort in the fact that professionals will keep your friend's struggle private and confidential.

SOMETIMES PARENTS AND EVEN FRIENDS AREN'T ENOUGH

Whether or not your friend responds to any of your help and whether or not he keeps using drugs, professionals need to step in. Without the help of professionals, motivating someone to stay away from drugs and keeping him from acquir-

Fighting addiction takes time and requires planning that will keep the recovering user from wanting to, or feeling resigned to, go back to that old habit.

ing more drugs is a difficult process. Substance abuse can take weeks, months, even years to overcome and can be exhausting to the recovering addict and to his support system. Expanding on that system is key. Unlike professionals, well-meaning parents and friends are not equipped to help kick a drug habit.

As you seek help, be careful not to betray your friend's trust. Rehabilitation is a private, sensitive matter, so don't share your knowledge of your friend's drug abuse by creating rumors to embarrass or hurt your friend among your peers. But be sure to let your friend's parents or guardians know if there is a drug problem, regardless of your friend's objections. Your friend's family has a right and a responsibility to know about the drug problem so they can then find appropriate avenues of support and treatment for your friend. Creating a social environment that has the purpose of easing the recovery process for your friend will help improve your friend's chances for success.

WHO CAN HELP?

Professionals who are ready to help with substance abuse are often found in places where many people typically go to seek help. Since drug addiction is a disease, doctors and psychologists are equipped to recognize and treat it. Drug abuse and addiction can impact the community of a school, so some social workers in a school environment must know what to do. And, since drug use can be considered a spiritual problem, religious counselors are often available to help in the rehabilitation process.

DOCTORS, PSYCHOLOGISTS, AND SOCIAL WORKERS

Medical doctors can identify the varying degrees of substance abuse in patients. They can offer strategies or suggest treatment options. In some cases, doctors prescribe medications to help ease intense withdrawal symptoms and to make it easier to wean a person off drugs.

Some psychologists or therapists specialize in substance abuse counseling. There are many different forms of therapy that are meant to help people fight substance abuse. One method is cognitive behavioral therapy (CBT), in which therapists help patients realize that harmful actions, thoughts, or emotions are not logical and rational. Through therapy sessions, patients learn to confront these emotions and develop self-help tools rather than turning to illicit drugs to make them feel better.

Social workers step in and help as counselors in hospitals, schools, shelters, and communities. They are familiar with resources such as rehabilitation centers, hospitals, and counseling centers that are available in the community. Social workers also help families cope with a teen who has been using drugs. They can help set up appointments, transport people to appointments or therapy sessions, and monitor the overall health and progress of a case.

CLERGY

Since 75 percent of Americans see themselves as religious or spiritual, it is common for drug users to seek help from clergy or pastors from their church. If your friend is religious, faith-based therapy might help. If a drug user meets with his church minister or with counselors in a faith-based therapy program, addressing the spiritual struggles that he is going through will also help him fight substance abuse. Faith-based counselors believe that drug users have a gap or a void in their lives that they are trying to fill with drugs. Faith-based counselors help the user turn to God or to their spirituality for help, in the hopes of filling the void and taking away the need for illicit drugs and addictive behavior.

WHAT'S THERAPY ALL ABOUT?

People who use drugs, as well as their family members, can turn to counseling or therapy for help. Therapy comes in

ALCOHOLICS ANONYMOUS

Alcoholics Anonymous is one organization that touches on faith and spirituality. Alcoholics Anonymous is free and utilizes a twelve-step program to help people overcome alcoholism. The twelve steps focus on these key tenets: acknowledging that the person is powerless over alcohol and that his life has become unmanageable; believing that a higher power or God will restore them to sanity and take care of them; searching for a personal moral inventory of oneself; admitting to wrongs and defects; and making amends to those who were wronged. Most people have a sponsor, someone who helps them every step of the way.

Since the 1930s, Alcoholics Anonymous has used prayer in its program. It is centered on faith and spirituality and developing and deepening one's connection to faith and God. If a person has a religious or spiritual belief system, AA might be an effective treatment path. If a person does not have religious or spiritual beliefs, AA might not be the right path to treatment.

Today, Alcoholics Anonymous serves people in 175 countries. It is estimated that there are more than two million people who use Alcoholics Anonymous to help them fight alcohol addiction.

many forms but usually therapists want to help people find solutions to their problems, overcome negative thoughts, empower themselves, and find tools for living without illicit drugs. Therapy usually includes individual sessions, group sessions, and/or residential treatment centers. The treatment plan is left to the team of professionals, the drug user, and the drug user's family.

INDIVIDUAL SESSIONS

One-on-one therapy sessions, or individual sessions, are private. Your friend will meet with a therapist. Individual sessions generally occur once or twice a week or once a month. A typical session lasts forty-five to sixty minutes.

Searching the internet or asking medical doctors for their recommendations are ways to find a qualified therapist. If any of your other friends have faced a drug problem, ask them if they can recommend a therapist. Your friend will want to find a therapist with whom he or she feels comfortable talking. A therapist is not a friend, but a counselor who will question, challenge, support, and motivate your friend.

The therapist may use cognitive behavioral therapy, psychoanalysis, or motivational therapy. The underlying theories behind these approaches include addressing negative or harmful behavior, addressing triggers that cause your friend to use drugs, setting goals for quitting, and finding ways to cope with stress and the substance abuse itself. Even though therapy is intended to help a person, the process requires honesty, self-reflection, and personal accountability. It will be a challenging emotional process for your friend.

GROUP THERAPY SESSIONS

Generally, group therapy involves one therapist and a group of people who are dealing with the same problem. Like in individual sessions, group members are sworn to confidentiality. Members are expected to listen to each other's struggles without passing judgement. They often help each other set reachable goals as they battle varying levels of substance abuse, including addiction. As certain individuals progress, they might serve as role models for other members.

Group therapy may seem unappealing because people don't like to share their secrets, fears, or weaknesses with total strangers. But, after trying group therapy, many people

A group of women have a discussion in an AA meeting. Support groups like this one help millions of people stay sober each year.

find that it is a supportive environment. They feel like they have found a group of close friends—all of whom are battling similar issues. People in the group cheer each other along and offer compassionate understanding when a person struggles. Group therapy is one of the most common treatment options, and it is often a part of a successful treatment plan.

Group sessions have additional benefits. They are typically more affordable than individual sessions with a therapist. Meetings can be held weekly, biweekly, or monthly. If a person has fully recovered, then that person may not need to attend any more group sessions. Or that person may be able to pop in and attend a session as needed.

Group therapy uses many methods to help people fight substance abuse and addiction—it is often more than just a discussion. If your friend begins a group therapy program, she might participate in art therapy, yoga, meditation, life-coaching, and life skills building.

RESIDENTIAL/IN-PATIENT THERAPY

An in-patient, or residential, treatment center may be most helpful if your friend is dealing with severe addiction and dependency. In-patient centers are usually recommended for people with a history of addiction and dependency. In-patient treatment centers are designed for people to live there while they get help. Most of the centers have thirty-, sixty-, or ninety-day treatment plans. The centers provide a team of specialists who offer medical care and therapy. Residential treatment programs are hard for most people in

The Elks Rehab Hospital is located in Boise, Idaho. Hospitals like this one, or residential treatment centers, are the most intensive ways to combat drug addiction.

recovery to endure. They are literally cut off from the rest of the world while they are in treatment. They will probably feel isolated and, often, betrayed. You can support your friend by not passing judgment and by being ready to offer support when he comes home.

CHAPTER FIVE

HELPING YOUR FRIEND STAY CLEAN

After your friend recognizes that he has a drug problem and gets help to fight it, the battle isn't over. Staying clean is tough. Stress, sadness, anxiety, and depression all might trigger your friend to have a relapse or return to using drugs.

Therapists recommend major lifestyle changes in order to beat drug problems. Therapists teach drug users how to avoid or cope with stress, how to avoid people and places where drugs are, and how to move on to a drug-free lifestyle.

DEALING WITH STRESS

Stress might trigger a recovering friend to crave an escape. Avoiding stress is ideal but not always possible. But when it arrives, there are ways to cope that don't involve relapsing.

AVOID STRESS

The best plan for a recovering drug abuser is to eliminate and avoid stress so that he isn't influenced to fall back into his old habits of drug abuse and addiction. Recovering addicts might feel stress because of others who pressure them to

Embarking on major lifestyle changes will offer a new perspective to someone who used to participate in different activities and hang out with different friends.

use drugs again. Or they might feel guilt or humiliation because they are afraid of what other people might think of them. Trying to win back old friends or make new ones is especially challenging during the process of recovering from a drug problem. One way to prevent stress in your friend's social circles is for your friend to be cognizant of how well he is adjusting. You can help with this by sharing your insights about how successful social interactions appear to be. You should help your friend recognize, in the case of considerably unsuccessful interactions, that he should let it go or seek further help before any trouble gets out of hand. If your friend's school performance has suffered from his substance abuse, making him aware of tutoring opportunities can offer an opportunity to catch up. Getting ahead of all of these issues, as well as others, can be very helpful in avoiding stress.

HEALTHY WAYS TO COPE WITH STRESS

If your friend can't avoid stress, help her find productive ways to cope with it.

Talking about stress is a good start to relieving it. Maybe you've been through something like what your friend is experiencing, and you know a good way of resolving the issue. Or maybe your friend doesn't want to feel alone and wants to make you understand what's going on or why something happened. If your friend's troubles present a burden that you feel is too big for you to deal with or keep a secret, consider which adults in your lives would be able to understand and help.

Taking care of one's health is a great way for someone to be prepared to cope with stress, starting with eating a balanced diet. What a person eats can have an impact on that person's mood. Many therapists recommend exercise. Exercise is a healthy way to relieve stress and burn off negative energy or anxiety. It also makes the body and the mind feel good because of the rush of endorphins, feel-good chemicals that circulate throughout your nervous system.

Taking breaks regularly can give a recovering addict some much-needed relief from a stressful task. In particular, connecting with nature can help someone who feels overwhelmed by life. Being surrounded by the natural beauty of trees in a park gives a sense of openness, and fresh air can have a calming effect. Being productive can also be helpful. Cleaning can be an activity for your friend to lose herself in her thoughts, or it can allow her to focus her energy and

TURNING TO ANIMALS

You've probably seen dogs used as therapy animals for people with posttraumatic stress disorder or dogs that visit people in hospitals. Now, therapists are capitalizing on a link between children, happiness, and pets. Therapy animals make people feel better. Scientists have found that just by petting an animal, stress levels drop in humans. Most people feel calmer, more relaxed, and happier in general around companion animals. Counselors think that animals, especially dogs and cats, might be able to distract or help humans tune out negative emotions and stress.

A pet might be able to help your friend overcome negative emotions or stress that he or she is dealing with while working to overcome a drug problem. By spending time petting a cat or taking a dog for a walk, your friend may feel better. Exercising by walking a dog is a healthy way to relieve stress. A pet can also be a great listener. Your friend can tell a dog anything, and it will never tell another soul or make fun of your friend.

mind on something that is not the cause of stress. A clean setting also allows one to focus more on whatever she is doing. Finally, social breaks can help someone to relax, as long as they are set up to be low-key and involve only a few people.

AVOID SITUATIONS WHERE DRUGS WILL BE

Take drugs out of the equation. Your friend knows where to go to find drugs, whether it's at a certain friend's party, in someone's home, or even at school. Know where those places are, too, so that you can help avoid those places and situations.

Just as your friend must avoid places, he must also avoid people. Many people who've used drugs begin to ditch old friends who aren't involved with drugs. Then, they start to hang out with other drug users and dealers. This way they can get their high easier, quicker, and without shame. Your friend must not continue to hang out with drug users and dealers, or she will be tempted to start using again.

In that vein, one key in recovering from a drug problem is to continue to work at the goal of hanging out with non–drug users. The hobbies or clubs your friend has joined or will join to occupy herself will now have the function of combatting stress and helping her cope with trigger situations, instead of just offering an alternative to drug use. In doing this, your friend will take her life back.

A BRIGHTER FUTURE

Once a friend starts using drugs, she's gone down a dangerous path. It is your role as a friend to help her see her behavior and recognize that she has a problem and then to be there to support her as she tries to get clean.

Just as recovering from severe substance abuse is exhausting, it is also exhausting to provide the support that someone needs. In the turmoil of your friend trying to improve

School activities like robotics club offer a healthy alternative to drug use. The skills a teen develops by learning engineering can serve her for a lifetime.

her health, it is important that you don't neglect yourself or the things you care about. If you begin to notice changes in your grades or relationships, that can be an indication that you don't have enough space to take care of your own responsibilities. Or it can mean that you're having trouble processing your feelings about what's happening. As you're navigating through your life, your friend needs to know and recognize your needs, too. It's your job to establish clear boundaries. Talk about what is and isn't acceptable behavior and what you need to function in your own life while you're offering support to your friend. While it is your friend's job to know what resources are available for her recovery, you must figure out and discuss what you need to maintain your own health.

GLOSSARY

ADDICTION A behavioral disease that causes someone to act obsessively toward obtaining a drug.

ASSAULT A violent attack on a person.

CONVULSIONS Involuntary jerking or shaking of the body.

COORDINATION The ability to control and move one's body; muscle and motor control.

DEPENDENCE A physiological need for a drug in order to function and prevent withdrawal.

DEPRESSION A condition of being sad, usually accompanied by a lack of interest and energy.

EMPOWER To give someone the tools to feel strong and in control of a situation.

EUPHORIC Feeling intense and extreme joy.

FLASHBACK A sudden memory of a past event or experience.

HALLUCINATIONS Visions of things or people that are not really there.

HIV Human immunodeficiency virus, the virus that can lead to AIDS.

HOMICIDE Murder.

ILLICIT Illegal, not allowed by the law.

NEUROTRANSMITTERS Substances in the body that carry messages from one nerve to another.

PERFORMANCE ENHANCERS Drugs, like steroids, that boost the physical performance of a person.

PSYCHOTIC Suffering from madness, loss of touch with reality.

PSYCHOANALYSIS A form of therapy that focuses on having the patient talk about dreams, past experiences, and feelings.

STDS Sexually transmitted diseases, including gonorrhea, syphilis, chlamydia, and herpes.

STIMULANT A drug or chemical that accelerates bodily functions and nervous system processing.

SUBSTANCE ABUSE The misuse or illegal use of any drug or excessive use of a legal drug.

SYNAPSES The places where one signal connects to another in a nerve cell.

SYNTHETIC Not natural, man-made by combining various substances and chemicals.

FOR MORE INFORMATION

Al-Anon/Alateen Family Group Headquarters, Inc.
1600 Corporate Landing Parkway
Virginia Beach, VA 23454-5617
(757) 563-1600
Website: http://al-anon.org/alateen-for-teens
Alateen is a large organization that helps teens who are battling alcohol addiction.

Al-Anon Family Group Headquarters (Canada) Inc.
275 Slater Street, Suite 900
Ottawa ON K1P 5H9
Canada
(613) 723-8484
Website: http://al-anon.org/for-alateen
Al-Anon Canada is a large organization that specializes in
helping people with alcohol addiction.

Drug Free America
Drug Free America Foundation, Inc.
5999 Central Avenue, Suite 301
Saint Petersburg, FL 33710
(727) 828-0211
Website: http://dfaf.org/
Drug Free America shares information about drug policy and
prevention in the United States.

Foundation for a Drug-Free World
1626 N. Wilcox Avenue, Suite 1297
Los Angeles, CA 90028
(888) 668-6378

Website: http://www.drugfreeworld.org/#/interactive
This is a nonprofit organization that educates students and
    parents from all over the world about drugs.

Office of Adolescent Health
1101 Wootton Parkway, Suite 700
Rockville, MD 20850
Website: http://www.hhs.gov/ash/oah/adolescent-health-topics
substance-abuse/home.html
The Office of Adolescent Health coordinates health-related
    programs through the U.S. Department of Health and Human
    Services. They provide detailed information on all aspects of
    teen health.

Partnership for a Drug-Free Canada
PO Box 23013
Toronto, ON M5N 38A
Canada
(416) 479-6972
Website: http://www.canadadrugfree.org/get-help/get-help-
    resources/
This organization is a Canadian charity that supplies information
    to parents in order to fight teenagers' drug problems.

Smart Recovery
7304 Mentor Avenue
Suite F
Mentor, OH 44060
(866) 951-5357
Website: http://www.smartrecovery.org/teens/
Smart Recovery is a training and self-management program
    for teens. They offer online message boards and other tools for
    teens in recovery.

Students Against Destructive Decisions (SADD)
255 Main Street
Marlborough, MA 01752
(877) SADD-INC
Website: http://www.sadd.org/who-we-are
SADD is an organization that empowers students to fight
  against drunk driving and addiction disorders.

WEBSITES

Because of the changing nature of internet links, Rosen
Publishing has developed an online list of websites related
to the subject of this book. This site is updated regularly.
Please use this link to access this list:

http://www.rosenlinks.com/HCIH/drug

FOR FURTHER READING

Conti, Nicolette, and Paula Johanson. *The Truth About Amphetamines and Stimulants.* New York, NY: Rosen Publishing, 2011.

Edelfield, Bruce, and Tracy Moosa. *Drug Abuse.* New York, NY: Rosen Publishing, 2011.

Friedman, Lauri. *Drug Abuse.* Detroit, MI: Greenhaven Press, 2012.

Friedman, Lauri. *Student Drug Testing.* Detroit, MI: Greenhaven Press, 2011.

Haugen, David. *Athletes and Drug Abuse.* Detroit, MI: Greenhaven Press, 2012.

Kimlan, Lanie, and Anne Alvergue. *The Truth About Ecstasy.* New York, NY: Rosen, 2011.

Latta, Sara. *Investigate: Steroids and Performance Drugs.* New York, NY: Enslow, 2014.

Marcovitz, Hal. *Diet Drugs.* Detroit, MI: Thomson Gale, 2007.

Menhard, Francha Roffé. *Drugs: The Facts About Inhalants.* Tarrytown, NY: Benchmark Books, 2005.

Merino, Noel. *Drug Legalization.* Detroit, MI: Greenhaven Press, 2015.

Merino, Noel. *Marijuana.* Detroit, MI: Greenhaven Press, 2011.

Muñoz, Mercedes, editor. *What Causes Addiction?* Detroit, MI: Greenhaven Press, 2005.

Naff, Clay Farris. *Nicotine and Tobacco.* San Diego, CA: Reference Point Press, 2007.

Rebman, Renee C. *Addictions and Risky Behaviors: Cutting, Bingeing, Snorting, and Other Dangers.* Berkeley Heights, NJ: Enslow, 2006.

Reynolds, Basia, and Jeremy Roberts. *The Truth About Prescription Drugs.* New York, NY: Rosen Publishing, 2011.

Roza, Greg. *The Encyclopedia of Drugs and Alcohol.* New York, NY: Franklin Watts, 2001.

Rubin, Julia. "How Heroin Is Invading America's Schools." *Teen Vogue,* September 10, 2013 (http://www.teenvogue.com/story/teen-heroin).

Stanmyre, Jackie. *Oxycodone.* New York, NY: Cavendish Square, 2015.

Waters, Rosa. *Over-the-Counter Medications.* Broomall, PA: Mason Crest, 2014.

Waters, Rosa. *Prescription Painkillers: OxyContin, Percocet, Vicodin & Other Addictive Analgesics.* Broomall, PA: Mason Crest, 2014.

BIBLIOGRAPHY

Addiction Center. "Teenage Drug Abuse and Addiction." December 18, 2015 (https://www.addictioncenter.com/teen-age-drug-abuse/).

Barter, James. *Hallucinogens.* San Diego, CA: Lucent Books, 2002.

Brown, Sarah Lennard. *Cocaine.* Chicago, IL: Raintree, 2005.

Brand, Russell. "My Life Without Drugs," *The Guardian,* March 9, 2013 (http://www.theguardian.com/culture/2013/mar/09/russell-brand-life-without-drugs).

Hazelden Betty Ford Foundation. "What Can I Say To Get You To Stop?" May 16, 2015 (http://www.hazeldenbettyford.org/articles/what-can-i-say-to-get-you-to-stop).

Himelstein, Rima. "Teen Heroin Use: An Unfortunate Reality." *The Inquirer Daily News,* September 10, 2013 (http://www.philly.com/philly/blogs/healthy_kids/Teen-heroin-use-an-unfortunate-reality.html).

Hyde, Margaret O., and John F. Setaro. *An Overview For Teens: Drugs 101.* Brookfield, CT: Twenty-First Century Books, 2003.

Landau, Elaine. *Meth: America's Drug Epidemic.* Minneapolis, MN: Lerner Publishing, 2008.

Menhard, Francha Roffé. *Drugs: The Facts About Inhalants.* Tarrytown, NY: Benchmark Books, 2005.

National Institute on Drug Abuse. "Drug Facts: High School and Youth Trends." December 2014 (https://www.drugabuse.gov/publications/drugfacts/high-school-youth-trends).

Project Know. "Teen Drug Addiction." 2016 (http://www.project-know.com/research/teen-drug-addiction/).

Recovery.org. "Find a Top Spiritual and Faith-Based Rehab Center." 2016 (http://www.recovery.org/topics/find-a-top-spiritual-and-faith-based-rehab-center/).

INDEX

A

alcohol, 10, 21, 24, 43
Alcoholics Anonymous, 43
amphetamines and metham-
   phetamines, 16-18, 35
anxiety, 8, 13, 14, 18, 48, 50
athletes, 16-17, 26-27, 31

B

boundary setting, 37, 53
brain function, 7, 35
butane hash oil (BHO), 12-13

C

casual drug use, 6
cocaine and crack cocaine, 14
cognitive behavioral therapy
   (CBT), 41

D

dependence, 7-8
depression, 8, 25, 48
drug use log, 31-32

E

experimentation, 6, 22-25

F

faith-based therapy, 41, 42

G

goal setting, 34
group therapy, 45-46

H

hallucinations, 9, 12, 14, 18,
   19
hallucinogens, 19, 35
Hazelden Betty Ford Foundation, 30, 37
heroin and opioids, 14-16, 17

I

inhalants, 13-14
intervention, 30-34

ABOUT THE AUTHOR

Precious McKenzie lives in Montana. She is an English professor at Rocky Mountain College. She has been an educator for over fifteen years. To unwind and have fun, McKenzie enjoys horseback riding, reading, and traveling.

PHOTO CREDITS: